NORM VAN BROCKLIN, MAR...
DAN TOWLER, ELROY HIRSCH, ISAAC
BRUCE, DAVID HILL, JACKIE SLATER,
ORLANDO PACE, TOM MACK, DENNIS
HARRAH, DOUG SMITH, DEACON JONES,
JACK YOUNGBLOOD, MERLIN OLSEN,
LARRY BROOKS, ISIAH ROBERTSON,
JACK REYNOLDS, LES RICHTER, LEROY
IRVIN, AENEAS

WILLIAMS, NOLAN

CROMWELL, JERRY GRAY, JEFF WILKINS,
DALE HATCHER, NORM VAN BROCKLIN,
MARSHALL FAULK, DAN TOWLER,
ELROY HIRSCH, ISAAC BRUCE, DAVID
HILL, JACKIE SLATER, ORLANDO PACE,

THE STORY OF THE LOS ANGELES RAMS

THE STORY OF THE
LOS ANGELES
RAMS

BY JIM WHITING

CREATIVE EDUCATION / CREATIVE PAPERBACKS

PUBLISHED BY CREATIVE EDUCATION AND CREATIVE PAPERBACKS
P.O. BOX 227, MANKATO, MINNESOTA 56002
CREATIVE EDUCATION AND CREATIVE PAPERBACKS ARE IMPRINTS OF THE
CREATIVE COMPANY
WWW.THECREATIVECOMPANY.US

DESIGN AND PRODUCTION BY BLUE DESIGN (WWW.BLUEDES.COM)
ART DIRECTION BY RITA MARSHALL
PRINTED IN CHINA

PHOTOGRAPHS BY ALAMY (EVERETT COLLECTION, INC.), CORBIS (BETTMANN),
GETTY IMAGES (ROB BROWN/NFL, MICHAEL BURR, KEVIN C. COX, WHITNEY
CURTIS, KEVORK DJANSEZIAN/STRINGER, JAY DROWNS, NATE FINE/NFL,
FOCUS ON SPORT, HARRY HOW, ROB LEITER, LONNIE MAJOR/ALLSPORT, JOHN
MCCOY/STRINGER, AL MESSERSCHMIDT/NFL, NFL, NFL PHOTOS, PRO FOOTBALL
HALL OF FAME, KEVIN REECE, JOE ROBBINS, BOB ROSATO/SI, VIC STEIN/NFL,
MATT SULLIVAN, TOM SZCZERBOWSKI, DILIP VISHWANAT)

NAMES: WHITING, JIM, AUTHOR.
TITLE: THE STORY OF THE LOS ANGELES RAMS / JIM WHITING.
SERIES: NFL TODAY.
INCLUDES INDEX.
SUMMARY: THIS HIGH-INTEREST HISTORY OF THE NATIONAL FOOTBALL
LEAGUE'S LOS ANGELES RAMS HIGHLIGHTS MEMORABLE GAMES, SUMMARIZES
SEASONAL TRIUMPHS AND DEFEATS, AND FEATURES STANDOUT PLAYERS SUCH
AS MERLIN OLSEN.
IDENTIFIERS: LCCN 2018035587 / ISBN 978-1-64026-147-1 (HARDCOVER) / ISBN
978-1-62832-710-6 (PBK) / ISBN 978-1-64000-265-4 (EBOOK)
SUBJECTS: LCSH: LOS ANGELES RAMS (FOOTBALL TEAM)—HISTORY—JUVENILE
LITERATURE. / FOOTBALL TEAMS—UNITED STATES—HISTORY—JUVENILE
LITERATURE.
CLASSIFICATION: LCC GV956.L6 W47 2019 / DDC 796.332/640979494—DC23

FIRST EDITION HC 9 8 7 6 5 4 3 2 1
FIRST EDITION PBK 9 8 7 6 5 4 3 2 1

COVER: TODD GURLEY
PAGE 2: JARED GOFF
PAGES 6-7: ROBERT QUINN, JAMES
LAURINAITIS, & BRADY POPPINGA

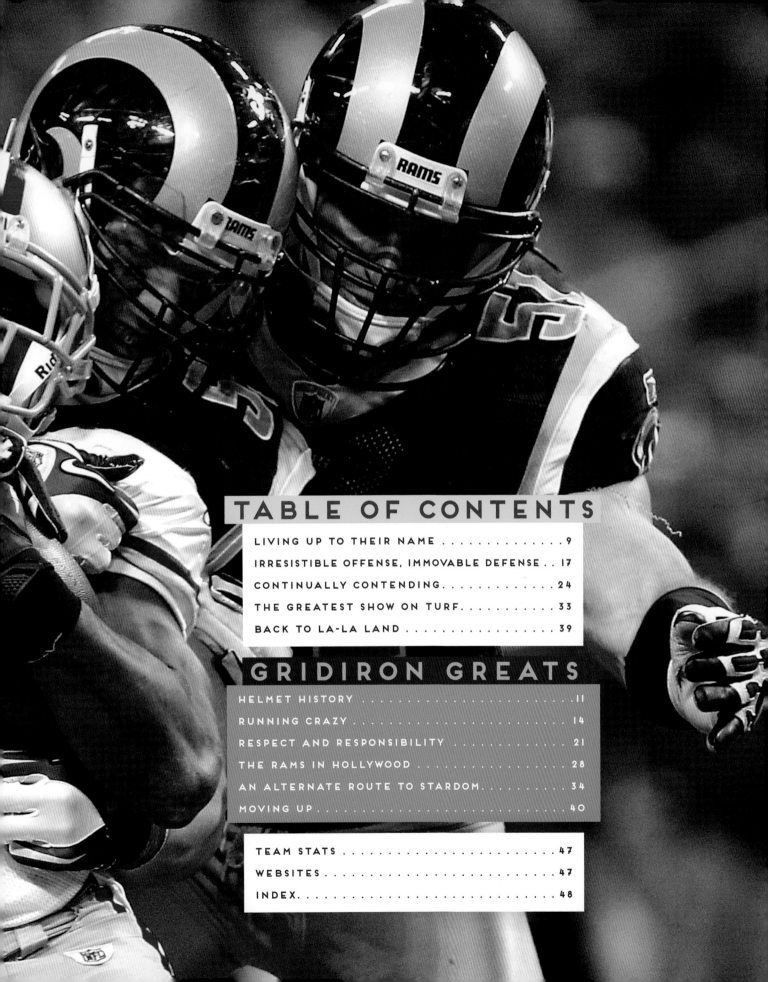

TABLE OF CONTENTS

GRIDIRON GREATS

LIVING UP TO THEIR NAME

In the 1930s, Fordham University in New York produced some of the best football teams in the country. The Fordham Rams were noted for their strong offensive line. These players were called the "Seven Blocks of Granite." Buzz Wetzel admired Fordham. Wetzel was general manager of a new National Football League (NFL) team. It was located in Cleveland, Ohio. He called his team the Rams. The name implied speed and power. Unfortunately, those qualities were lacking when the team began play in 1937. Their college namesake went 7–0–1 that season. The Fordham Rams were ranked third in the country. But Cleveland finished at a woeful 1–10.

In 1939, Cleveland went 5–5–1. Rookie quarterback Parker Hall led the league in completions. He earned the Most Valuable Player (MVP) award. Aside from that season, the Rams posted losing records. It took another rookie to spark the team in 1945. The story was practically a Hollywood script. The rookie was quarterback Bob "The Rifle" Waterfield. Like Hall, Waterfield was named the league's MVP. He led the Rams to a 9–1 season. Cleveland topped its division.

The Rams hosted the Washington Redskins for the 1945 NFL Championship Game. A blizzard blew into Cleveland. The game-day temperature dropped to -2 °F (-18.9 °C). In the first quarter, Washington quarterback Sammy Baugh threw a pass from his own end zone. The ball hit the goalpost. It bounced to the frozen turf. Under existing rules, it was a safety. The Rams received two points. In the end, those points decided the game. Each team scored two touchdowns. Washington made both extra points. The Rams missed one. But they held on to win. A sportswriter gave Waterfield credit for the win. "Waterfield literally beat the Washington Redskins 15–14, singlehanded," he wrote.

Owner Dan Reeves rewarded Waterfield with a new

LEFT: BOB WATERFIELD

GRIDIRON GREATS v
HELMET HISTORY

Until 1948, all NFL players wore plain leather helmets. Rams halfback Fred Gehrke had been an art major in college. He painted golden-yellow ram's horns on the team's headgear. Owner Dan Reeves paid him $1 per helmet. Making one for every player took him several months. When the Rams wore them for the first time, everyone in the stands leaped to their feet. Fans applauded the new look. Other teams quickly added designs to their helmets. Today, all NFL teams except the Cleveland Browns display logos on their helmets.

LOS ANGELES RAMS

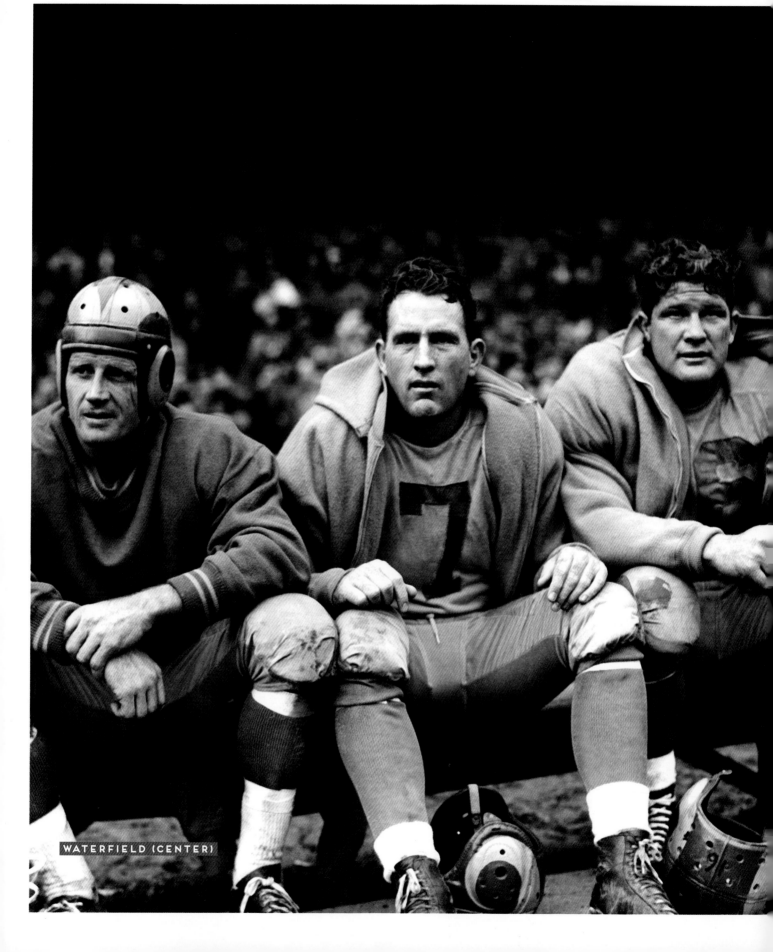

WATERFIELD (CENTER)

"WATERFIELD LITERALLY BEAT THE WASHINGTON REDSKINS 15-14, SINGLEHANDED."

contract. It paid him $20,000 a year. That was far more than any other player received. A New York native, Reeves wasn't happy with Cleveland. He had purchased the Rams in 1941. He kept losing money on them. In addition, another Cleveland team was about to begin play. That team was called the Browns. Much of the roster consisted of Ohio State players. The coach was local hero Paul Brown. So Reeves announced plans to move the team to Los Angeles. World War II had just ended. The Southern California area was booming. Reeves felt that he would attract more spectators there. At that point, no city west of the Mississippi River had been home to an NFL team. Other NFL owners expressed concern. They thought it might cost too much to travel to the West Coast for games. Still, the move was approved.

GRIDIRON GREATS ∨
RUNNING CRAZY

Elroy Hirsch was nicknamed "Crazylegs." He earned it while playing high school football. When he ran, his legs appeared to whirl in several directions at once. "Elroy ran to school and back, skipping and crisscrossing his legs in the cement blocks of the sidewalks," his father said. "He said it would make him shiftier." When he joined the Rams, Hirsch gained attention with his ability to catch long-distance bombs from quarterbacks Bob Waterfield and Norm Van Brocklin. Hirsch displayed a unique catching style, too. He grabbed the ball with his fingertips while running at full speed. It became known as the "Elroy Hirsch Special."

63 CAREER TOUCHDOWNS

127 GAMES PLAYED

IRRESISTIBLE OFFENSE, IMMOVABLE DEFENSE

n 1946, the Los Angeles Rams made history again. The team signed halfback Kenny Washington and end Woody Strode. They were the first black NFL players in 14 years. In 1949, Los Angeles went 8-2-2. It won the NFL's West Division. One reason was Tom Fears. "Fears was one of the greatest 'move' men in the history of the game," said coach Sid Gillman. "He didn't have much speed, but he could turn 'em on their heads." Fears led the league with 77 receptions. He teamed up with fellow ends Elroy "Crazylegs" Hirsch and

LOS ANGELES RAMS

COACH GEORGE ALLEN

Bob Shaw. They formed the three-receiver spread forma-
tion. It revolutionized the passing game. The Rams had
one of the best offenses in the league.

The Rams hosted the Philadelphia Eagles in the 1949
NFL Championship Game. Heavy rains flooded Los
Angeles Memorial Coliseum. The field was a muddy mess.
The Eagles dominated the game. The Rams failed to score.
They lost, 0–14. The next year, Los Angeles was a scoring
machine. The Rams featured three bruising fullbacks
in the backfield. They were "Deacon Dan" Towler, Dick
Hoerner, and Tank Younger. Each man weighed about
225 pounds. The group was called the "Bull Elephant
Backfield." It gave the Rams a fearsome running game.
Against the Baltimore Colts, Los Angeles scored 70 points.
In total, the Rams scored 466 regular-season points in
1950. It was a league record. Unfortunately, they lost in
the NFL Championship Game. The Cleveland Browns
pulled out the win on a field goal with 28 seconds left.

Quarterback Norm Van Brocklin had been drafted
in 1949. He soon began splitting playing time
with Waterfield. In 1951, the Rams returned to the
championship game. Van Brocklin launched a 73-yard
touchdown pass to Fears late in the fourth quarter.
The score put the Rams over the Browns. It secured
the title. In 1955, the Rams made another run for the

LOS ANGELES RAMS

208

208 GAMES PLAYED

14

14 CONSECUTIVE PRO BOWL APPEARANCES

GRIDIRON GREATS ∨
RESPECT AND
RESPONSIBILITY

Players and fans alike looked up to Merlin Olsen. He was a big guy. He was also a smart leader and a dependable player. During his 15-year career, he was one of the best defensive tackles in the league. When he retired, he was the Rams' all-time leading tackler. Olsen racked up 915 stops. He was part of the "Fearsome Foursome." The quartet's popularity sparked interest among NFL fans in the defensive side of football. Olsen set a hardworking example for his teammates. "The winning team has a dedication," he said. "It will have at its core a group of veteran players who set the standards. They will not accept defeat."

21

[SACK] DESCRIBED TACKLING THE PASSER BEHIND THE LINE OF SCRIMMAGE…. "YOU KNOW, YOU SACK A CITY—YOU DEVASTATE IT."

—DEACON JONES

championship. But the Browns beat them, 38–14. After that, the good times faded. The Rams enjoyed only one winning season in the next decade.

Defensive end David "Deacon" Jones joined the team in 1961. He became one of the most intimidating pass rushers in NFL history. The following year, the Rams drafted Merlin Olsen. He was a burly defensive tackle. Jones and Olsen brought glamour and excitement to the defensive side of the ball. They joined forces with tackle Rosey Grier and end Lamar Lundy. The group became known as the "Fearsome Foursome." They made life miserable for opposing quarterbacks. But fans loved them. Jones coined the term "sack." This described tackling the passer behind the line of scrimmage. "We needed a shorter term," he said. "Like, you know, you sack a city—you devastate it."

MERLIN OLSEN (NUMBER 74)
AND DEACON JONES (75)

CONTINUALLY CONTENDING

Los Angeles compiled a 32–7–3 record from 1967 through 1969. The team topped its division twice. The Super Bowl had become part of the NFL in 1966. The Rams were unable to reach it. But the team remained strong. From 1973 to 1979, Los Angeles topped the National Football Conference (NFC) West Division each year. During the 1970s, the Rams' defense allowed fewer total yards and fewer points than any other team in the NFL. Its heart was end Jack Youngblood. He was tough and persistent.

RUNNING BACK ERIC DICKERSON

In 1979, Youngblood broke his leg during a playoff game against the Dallas Cowboys. Team trainers taped him up. Then he returned to the game. He sacked Cowboys quarterback Roger Staubach in the fourth quarter. "Got me a sack on a cracked leg," he said. "There may not be too many guys who can say that!" One week later, Youngblood was back. He wore a leg brace in the NFC Championship Game against the Tampa Bay Buccaneers. The Rams kicked three field goals. That was all they needed. They won, 9–0. Then they faced the Pittsburgh Steelers in Super Bowl XIV. Unfortunately, Youngblood's grit could not carry the Rams to victory. The Rams led 19–17 after three quarters. But the Steelers pulled away to win, 31–19.

TARZAN... trapped by the erupting volcano!

GRIDIRON GREATS v
THE RAMS IN HOLLYWOOD

A number of Rams players took advantage of their proximity to Hollywood. Bob Waterfield was married to actress Jane Russell. The couple had a movie production company. Elroy Hirsch played himself in the 1953 movie *Crazylegs.* He also appeared in the films *Unchained* (1955) and *Zero Hour!* (1957). Linebacker Mike Henry found Hollywood success, too. He took the role of Tarzan in the 1960s. During the 1970s, Merlin Olsen played Jonathan Garvey in the television series *Little House on the Prairie*. Defensive end Fred Dryer was a key member of the Rams' defense in the 1970s. Years later, he starred in the television detective series *Hunter*.

The Rams hit a low point in 1982. A players' strike cut the season short. The team won just two games. It finished at the bottom of the NFC. By the next year, the Rams were on the rise. Running back Eric Dickerson smashed the NFL rookie rushing record. He ran for 1,808 yards. "He made no noise when he ran," said coach John Robinson. "If you were blind, he could run right by you, and I don't think you'd know he was there unless you felt the wind."

LINEBACKER/END KEVIN GREENE

JIM EVERETT

T hree years later, Dickerson was traded to the Indianapolis Colts. Quarterback Jim Everett kept the team on the winning track. In 1988, he led the NFL with 31 touchdown passes. Many went to receiver Henry Ellard. Everett guided his team to 11 wins in 1989. In the playoffs, the Rams charged past the Eagles and New York Giants. They faced the San Francisco 49ers for the NFC championship. The game represented the Rams' decade of hope and disappointment. San Francisco crushed them, 30–3.

MARSHALL FAULK

THE GREATEST SHOW ON TURF

After that, the Rams posted losing records for a number of years. Attendance waned. The team struggled to find support for a new stadium. Owner Georgia Frontiere moved the team to St. Louis for the 1995 season. For the Rams' opening home game, nearly 60,000 fans packed Busch Stadium. The Rams rewarded them by winning their first four games. Then, they slid into a losing streak. They finished 7–9. They endured three more losing seasons in St. Louis.

The Rams needed a boost. So they traded for running back Marshall Faulk in 1999. He was famous for his agility. "He can go from a standing start to full speed faster than anybody I've ever seen," said former coach Ted Marchibroda. Faulk could catch passes, too. St. Louis also drafted speedy receiver Torry Holt. The roster looked promising. But quarterback

KURT WARNER
QUARTERBACK

KURT WARNER
QUARTERBACK

RAMS SEASONS: 1998–2003
HEIGHT: 6-FOOT-2
WEIGHT: 220 POUNDS

GRIDIRON GREATS
AN ALTERNATE ROUTE TO STARDOM

Kurt Warner played quarterback for the University of Northern Iowa. He had a solid college career. But the small school didn't attract much NFL attention. No team drafted Warner. The following year, Des Moines fielded a team called the Barnstormers. It was part of the Arena Football League (AFL). Warner took full advantage of the opportunity. In 1997, he completed 65 percent of his passes. He threw 79 touchdowns. The NFL finally took notice. Warner signed with the Rams in 1998. One season later, he led the team to its first Super Bowl victory. He was inducted into the Hall of Fame in 2017.

124

124 GAMES PLAYED

208

208 CAREER PASSING TOUCHDOWNS

Trent Green hurt his knee before the season started. The injury kept him out for the year. Green's backup was Kurt Warner. He had little NFL experience. Few people knew who he was. It didn't take long for Warner to silence his critics. The Rams offense exploded. It became known as "The Greatest Show on Turf." Warner threw a whopping 41 touchdown passes. He led St. Louis to a 13–3 record. "I told our team we could win with Kurt," said coach Dick Vermeil. "I didn't expect … that we'd win *because* of him."

In the postseason, the Rams toppled the Minnesota Vikings and the Buccaneers. They faced the Tennessee Titans in Super Bowl XXXIV. The game was tied late in the fourth quarter. Then Warner threw a touchdown strike to receiver Isaac Bruce. On the final play of the game, the Titans had the ball deep in St. Louis territory. But Rams linebacker Mike Jones stopped Tennessee one yard short of the goal line. The game was over. St. Louis won, 23–16. The Rams claimed their first Super Bowl win!

The Rams charged back in 2001. They finished with 14 wins. It was the best record in team history. The Rams defeated the Green Bay Packers and the Philadelphia Eagles in the playoffs. This brought them face-to-face with the New England Patriots in Super Bowl XXXVI. The game turned out to be a nail-biter. With 90 seconds remaining, Warner threw a touchdown pass to receiver Ricky Proehl. The score was tied at 17. In the final seconds, New England booted a 48-yard field goal. The Patriots won.

Warner broke a finger in 2002. He missed several games. When he did play, he struggled. He threw just 3 touchdowns and racked up 11 interceptions. The Rams skidded to 7–9. Backup quarterback Marc Bulger took over. The Rams led the NFC West in 2003. The next year, bruising rookie running back Steven Jackson helped St. Louis return to the playoffs. The Rams topped the Seattle Seahawks. But the Atlanta Falcons crushed St. Louis a week later, 47–17.

STEVEN JACKSON

BACK TO LA-LA LAND

T he Rams' championship window closed after the 2004 season. The team dropped to 6–10 in 2005. It improved slightly in 2006. But it plummeted to 3–13 the following year. The Rams kept sinking. They won just two games in 2008. They managed only one victory in 2009.

In 2010, the Rams chose quarterback Sam Bradford in the NFL Draft. Bradford played every snap in his first season. With his help, the Rams dramatically increased their scoring. Their defense improved, too. The team entered its final game of the regular season

GRIDIRON GREATS v
MOVING UP

In 2010, Rivals.com rated Aaron Donald the 37th-best high school defensive tackle in the country. By now, he has surpassed the 36 players who ranked ahead of him. He became NFL Defensive Rookie of the Year in 2014. He was named First-Team All-Pro the next four seasons. In 2017, he became the first interior lineman in 18 years to be voted Defensive Player of the Year. In 2018, he led the league with 20.5 quarterback sacks and was again named Defensive Player of the Year. Seahawks quarterback Russell Wilson called him "the best defensive player I've ever played against."

AARON DONALD
DEFENSIVE TACKLE

RAMS SEASONS: 2014-PRESENT
HEIGHT: 6-FOOT-1
WEIGHT: 280 POUNDS

LOS ANGELES RAMS

with a record of 7–8. It faced the Seahawks. The winning team would make the playoffs. The loser would be out. Unfortunately, the Rams' offense never got on track. Seattle won, 16–6.

The offense sputtered again in 2011. The Rams finished with two wins. They continued to compile losing records. One of the few bright spots was defensive tackle Aaron Donald. He was Defensive Rookie of the Year in 2014. Running back Todd Gurley was another highlight. He ran for 1,106 yards in 2015. He was named Offensive Rookie of the Year.

In 2016, the Rams returned to Los Angeles. They stumbled to 4–12. New coach Sean McVay turned the team around in 2017. Hired at age 30, he was the youngest head coach in NFL history. The Rams surged to 11–5. They won the NFC West for the first time in 14 years. The season included a 42–7 road win over the Seahawks. Seattle had dominated the division for a number of years. It was

LEFT: LINEBACKER JAMES LAURINAITIS

WIDE RECEIVER DANNY AMENDOLA

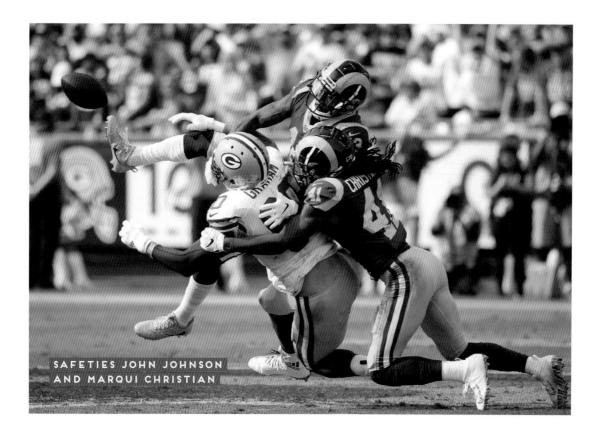

SAFETIES JOHN JOHNSON
AND MARQUI CHRISTIAN

considered almost unbeatable at home. Unfortunately, the Rams lost to the Falcons in the playoffs. But Gurley was voted Offensive Player of the Year. Donald was Defensive Player of the Year. Young quarterback Jared Goff gave promise of a solid career. After a 13–3 season in 2018, the Rams clinched the NFC championship to face the Patriots in the Super Bowl. But the Pats defeated them, 13–3.

After a shaky start in the 1930s, the Rams have nimbly navigated the NFL. They have won championships in Cleveland, Los Angeles, and St. Louis. Today, fans are happy that the team has returned to the City of the Angels. They hope it will be the starting point for many more successful seasons.

NFL CHAMPIONSHIPS

1945, 1951, 1999

WEBSITES

LOS ANGELES RAMS

https://www.therams.com/

NFL: LOS ANGELES RAMS TEAM PAGE

http://www.nfl.com/teams/losangelesrams/profile?team=LA

LOS ANGELES RAMS

INDEX

DEFENSIVE END
CHRIS LONG